Dinosaur

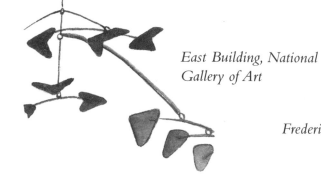

East Building, National
Gallery of Art

Frederick Douglass
House

Inaugural Gown

First Woman US Supreme Court Justice

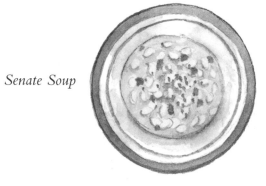

"Necessary,"
Mount Vernon

Owney,
Postal Service
Mascot

Pentagon

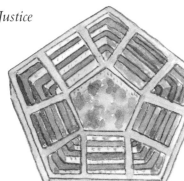
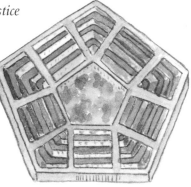

Senate Soup

Teddy Bear

Xmas Time

Yummy!

Zschock

American Beauty

Bird

*Carousel,
Glen Echo Park*

*Giant,
Haines Point*

Hopscotch

Kite Festival

*Lichtenstein,
Sculpture Garden*

Mary McLeod Bethune

Quill Pen

Row House

Uncle Sam

Vendor

*West Building,
National Gallery
of Art*

Journey Around

Washington, D.C.

from A to Z

Martha Day Zschock

COMMONWEALTH EDITIONS

Carlisle, Massachusetts

*To my wonderful family
and to the good ol' red, white, and blue!*

*And a hip hip hooray for . . . Webster and Katie Bull, Penny Stratton,
Elizabeth Muller, Gary Scott at the National Park Service, our friends at Jay's,
and Capt. Charles Zschock, tour guide extraordinaire!*

Copyright © 2004 by Martha Zschock. All rights reserved.
Designed by Heather Zschock

No part of this book may be reproduced in any form
without written permission from the publisher.
Commonwealth Editions
An Imprint of Applewood Books, Inc.
Carlisle, Massachusetts 01741
Visit us at www.commonwealtheditions.com.

Visit Martha Zschock at www.marthazschock.com.

ISBN 978-1-889833-62-0

10 9 8 7 6

Printed in the U.S.A.

GREETINGS, MY FRIENDS, AND

Welcome to Washington, D.C.!

PEOPLE TRAVEL FROM ALL PARTS of the country and the world to visit America's capital city and "hometown," Washington, D.C. Bordered by Maryland and Virginia, the city is home to the U.S. federal government. Its buildings, monuments, and people are a tribute to the country's history, culture, and commitment to democracy.

Ratified in 1788, the U.S. Constitution allowed for the creation of a permanent home for the government, which previously had met in New York, Philadelphia, and Princeton, New Jersey. George Washington chose the area that is now Washington, D.C., and enlisted Pierre Charles L'Enfant to create a grand design for the new capital city. L'Enfant envisioned broad avenues radiating from the U.S. Capitol, the crowning jewel of the city. His plan is the underlying structure of today's bustling capital.

Despite some major setbacks, the city continued to grow and develop. Its unconquerable spirit mirrors the determination of the nation as a whole. Today this energetic city is filled with government buildings, museums dedicated to education and the preservation of American heritage and culture, monuments to those who have devoted their lives to serving their country—and lots of fun!

Come, there's much to explore. Let's take a journey around Washington, D.C.!

America's
Anthem
awakens awe.

Francis Scott Key was inspired to write "The Star Spangled Banner," America's national anthem, during the War of 1812 when he saw the U.S. flag flying triumphantly over Fort McHenry. The family of Major George Armistead, the fort's commander, cherished the flag for almost a century. In 1907, they gave it to the Smithsonian Institution, to be displayed and preserved. The flag and the song fill people's hearts with pride.

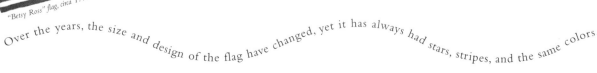

Over the years, the size and design of the flag have changed, yet it has always had stars, stripes, and the same colors.

Circa 1818

"Betsy Ross" flag, circa 1777

"Fillmore" flag, circa 1777

Star Spangled Banner,
National Museum of American History
Inset: Washington Redskins and fans
Details: Evolution of the American flag

Boats paddle
by Basin
blossoms.

CHERRY BLOSSOM
King & Queen

EVERY SPRING, approximately one million people stroll along the Tidal Basin to see thousands of magnificent cherry trees in bloom. The beloved trees were a gift of friendship from Japan in 1912. Each year Park Service experts try to predict when the buds will pop, hoping it will be during the annual Cherry Blossom Festival. The nearby Thomas Jefferson Memorial is a tribute to the country's third president and author of the Declaration of Independence.

Jefferson diphylla, wildflower named after Jefferson in honor of his knowledge of natural beauty

Jefferson Memorial, Tidal Basin
Inset: Cherry Blossom Festival parade
Detail: *Jeffersonia diphylla*

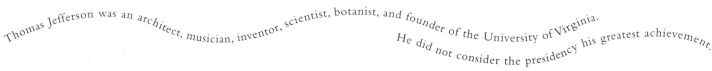

Thomas Jefferson was an architect, musician, inventor, scientist, botanist, and founder of the University of Virginia. He did not consider the presidency his greatest achievement.

Congress convenes in Capitol chambers.

THE U.S. CAPITOL HOUSES CONGRESS, the legislative branch of government. Consisting of the Senate and the House of Representatives, Congress is responsible for creating the laws that govern the country. The original design of the building has grown along with the nation since George Washington laid the cornerstone in 1793. The spectacular Rotunda connects the building's two sides, and an underground subway transports congressmen and women to and from their offices.

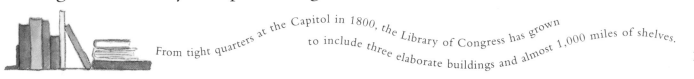

From tight quarters at the Capitol in 1800, the Library of Congress has grown to include three elaborate buildings and almost 1,000 miles of shelves.

U.S. Capitol
Inset: The Rotunda
Details: Library of Congress

Drama, dance, and music delight the District.

ALL THE WORLD'S A STAGE AND ALL THE MEN AND WOMEN MERELY PLAYERS

THE KENNEDY CENTER, a memorial to the 35th president, has several theaters and hosts over 3,000 music, dance, and theater performances a year. Its Millennium Stage offers free shows daily. The Smithsonian's Discovery Theater entertains and teaches children through puppetry, dance, and storytelling. Folks can enjoy outdoor summer performances at the Ellipse, on the National Mall, and outside the city at Wolf Trap Farm Park.

John F. Kennedy Center for the Performing Arts
Inset: Discovery Theater
Detail: William Shakespeare

The Elizabethan Theater at the Folger Shakespeare Library brings plays by William Shakespeare to life in an authentic setting.

Emancipation established equality.

ABRAHAM LINCOLN BELIEVED that all people are created equal. When he became president in 1861, several southern states broke away from the Union over the issue of slavery. In 1863, during the Civil War, Lincoln issued the Emancipation Proclamation, which said that slaves would be free in states that had left the Union. Finally, in 1865, the 13th Amendment to the Constitution ended slavery in the entire country.

Even though slavery was abolished, the road to equality has been long for African Americans, whose rights have been granted one step at a time.

Lincoln Memorial
Inset: Reflecting Pool
Detail: Martin Luther King Jr.'s "I Have a Dream" speech, 1963

Founders fought for freedom.

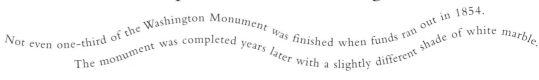

GEORGE WASHINGTON has been called the Father of Our Country because of his leadership during times of war and peace. During the Revolutionary War, he was commander in chief of the Continental Army, helping the colonies win independence from Britain. After the war, he helped form the new U.S. government and became the first president. The Washington Monument, standing tall at the heart of the capital, is a tribute to his greatness.

Washington Monument
Inset: Washington's uniform, National Museum of American History
Detail: Washington Monument under construction

Not even one-third of the Washington Monument was finished when funds ran out in 1854. The monument was completed years later with a slightly different shade of white marble.

THE STRANGE GARGOYLES watching over Washington National Cathedral are actually water-spouts that carry rain away from the building. The cathedral was created as a church for all people and is decorated with symbols of America's religious and national heritage. Work on the ornate gothic building began in 1907 and took exactly 83 years to complete.

The cathedral has a chapel designed especially for children. It is fancifully decorated with baby animals.

Gargoyle outside Washington National Cathedral
Inset: Washington National Cathedral
Details: Children's Chapel

Heroes and heroines soar with high hopes.

THROUGHOUT HISTORY, people have dreamed of flying, but it is only a little more than one hundred years since the Wright Brothers first flew a powered airplane, launching the age of flight. From wobbly gliders to missions in space, the technological advances during the first century of flight have been remarkable. Brave pioneers have opened a universe of possibilities to future explorers, for whom the sky truly is the limit.

Wright Brothers' Plane, National Air and Space Museum
Inset: Space window, Washington National Cathedral
Details: Hot-air balloon, National Air and Space Museum

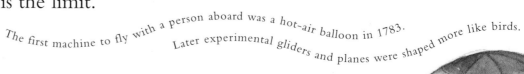

The first machine to fly with a person aboard was a hot-air balloon in 1783.
Later experimental gliders and planes were shaped more like birds.

I mprovements
inspired
imaginations.

PRESIDENT FRANKLIN D. ROOSEVELT's strong character, courage, and optimism helped lead the nation through troubled times. His "New Deal" created jobs, opportunities, and hope during the Great Depression. Before the country entered World War II, FDR reminded the nation of the "Four Freedoms" we must fight for: freedoms of speech and worship, and freedoms from want and fear. He encouraged Americans with his "fireside chats," broadcast by radio.

Polio left FDR in a wheelchair at age 39. Today he is admired for his invincible spirit in the face of physical challenges.

Hunger, Franklin D. Roosevelt Memorial
Inset: Fala, FDR's dog, FDR Memorial
Detail: FDR statue

Justices join in judgment.

THE SUPREME COURT is the judicial branch of the government. The president appoints the nine justices (one chief justice and eight associate justices) for life. The Court is responsible for making sure that our nation's laws follow the principles of the U.S. Constitution.

Its motto, carved on the front of the Supreme Court building, is "Equal Justice Under Law." The justices shake hands with one another as a reminder to work together for this purpose.

U.S. Supreme Court
Inset: Supreme Court chamber
Detail: Tortoise inside Supreme Court building

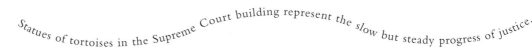

Statues of tortoises in the Supreme Court building represent the slow but steady progress of justice.

Kudos to those who kept the tracks.

WASHINGTON, D.C.'S GRAND UNION STATION opened in 1908, replacing an old neighborhood known as "Swampoodle." It became a major transportation hub serving the District for over half a century until air travel became more popular and the building fell into decline. A restoration project completed in 1988 returned the building to its original splendor, adding shops, restaurants, and a movie theater, and bringing in the city's clean and efficient Metro subway trains.

Ronald Reagan National Airport is the closest of D.C.'s three nearby airports. Visitors arriving by car must cross the Beltway, the highway that circles the city.

Union Station
Inset: Metro train
Detail: Ronald Reagan National Airport

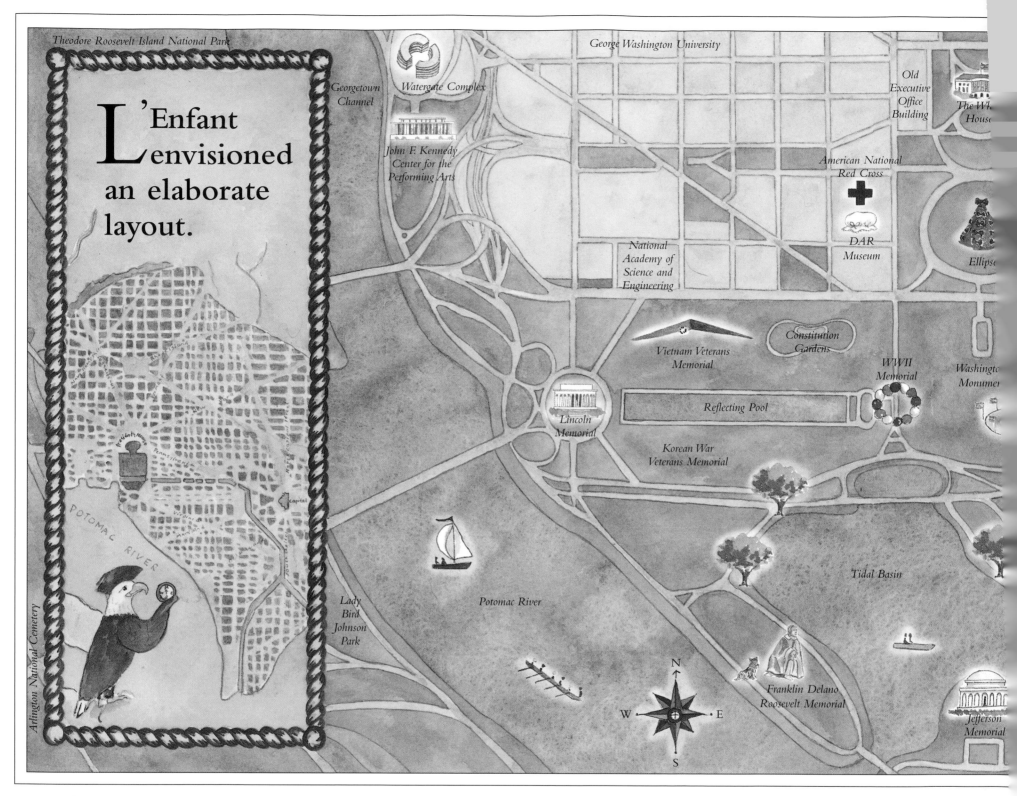

Theodore Roosevelt Island National Park

George Washington University

Old Executive Office Building

The White House

L'Enfant L envisioned an elaborate layout.

Georgetown Channel

Watergate Complex

John F. Kennedy Center for the Performing Arts

American National Red Cross

DAR Museum

Ellipse

National Academy of Science and Engineering

Vietnam Veterans Memorial

Constitution Gardens

WWII Memorial

Washington Monument

Reflecting Pool

Lincoln Memorial

Korean War Veterans Memorial

POTOMAC RIVER

Lady Bird Johnson Park

Potomac River

Tidal Basin

Arlington National Cemetery

N
W E
S

Franklin Delano Roosevelt Memorial

Jefferson Memorial

AFTER THE REVOLUTIONARY WAR, a temporary government met in New York and Philadelphia to draft the new country's constitution. After a few revisions, it was ratified in 1788. George Washington was chosen to be the first president the following year. He soon set about creating a permanent home for the capital that would be separate from any state, as the Constitution provided.

Washington, D.C., from the Capitol to the Potomac
Inset: L'Enfant's original vision for the city
Detail Left: Pierre Charles L'Enfant

L'Enfant, who left the project after a year, is buried in Arlington National Cemetery, on a hill overlooking the city.

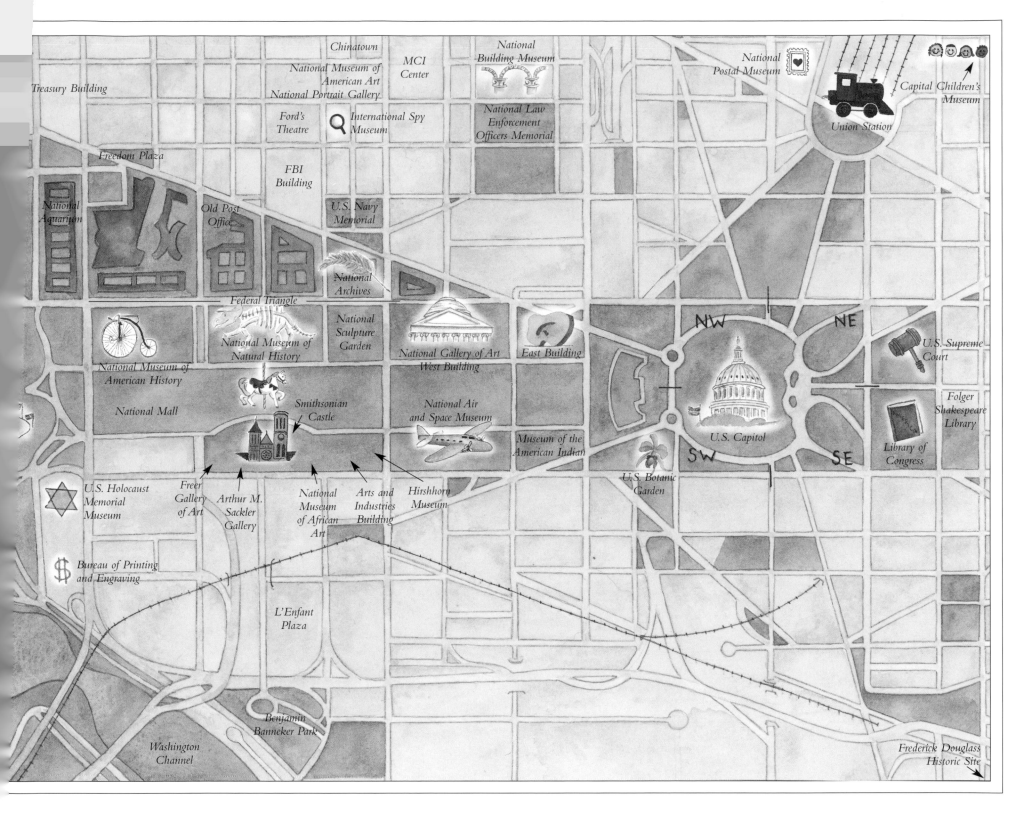

Chinatown

National Museum of American Art
National Portrait Gallery

MCI Center

National Building Museum

National Postal Museum

Capital Children's Museum

Treasury Building

Ford's Theatre

International Spy Museum

National Law Enforcement Officers Memorial

Union Station

Freedom Plaza

FBI Building

U.S. Navy Memorial

National Aquarium

Old Post Office

National Archives

Federal Triangle

National Sculpture Garden

National Museum of Natural History

National Gallery of Art West Building

East Building

NW

NE

U.S. Supreme Court

National Museum of American History

National Mall

Smithsonian Castle

National Air and Space Museum

Museum of the American Indian

U.S. Capitol

SW

SE

Folger Shakespeare Library

Library of Congress

U.S. Holocaust Memorial Museum

Freer Gallery of Art

Arthur M. Sackler Gallery

National Museum of African Art

Arts and Industries Building

Hirshhorn Museum

U.S. Botanic Garden

Bureau of Printing and Engraving

L'Enfant Plaza

Benjamin Banneker Park

Washington Channel

Frederick Douglass Historic Site

A DIAMOND-SHAPED AREA between Virginia and Maryland was chosen to become the U.S. capital. Pierre Charles L'Enfant, the city's chief planner, developed grand designs for the Capitol on Jenkins Hill and a broad avenue leading to the White House. Divided into four sections with the Capitol at the center, today's Washington, D.C., resembles L'Enfant's original design.

Andrew Ellicott and Benjamin Banneker took over the job of laying out the city's streets and parks, preserving L'Enfant's original design.

Planning the city

Money machines manufacture millions.

(Inset $10 bill annotations):
Teeny tiny words
Fine line patterns are hard to copy
There's a hidden security thread that says "USA TEN"—hold the bill up to the light!
color shifting ink
Held up to the light, there's a hidden portrait here.

THE BUREAU OF ENGRAVING AND PRINTING prints millions of dollars each day, along with stamps, government documents, and White House invitations. Visitors can dream as they watch money being printed, inspected, sorted, and cut. Every seven to ten years, notes are redesigned to discourage counterfeiting. "NexGen" currency, first issued in the fall of 2003, is more colorful than the traditional green bills.

Bureau of Engraving and Printing
Inset: Security features of a $10 bill
Details: Start saving!

The Bureau of Printing and Engraving prints only paper money (currency). Coins are minted in New York, Denver, San Francisco, and Philadelphia.

Native bounty abounds at neighborhood markets.

EASTERN MARKET, built behind Capitol Hill in 1873, is the oldest continually operated fresh food public market in Washington, D.C. The market was badly damaged by fire in 2007, but determined merchants kept the operation running, selling their wares outside and in a temporary annex while renovations were underway. Reopened in 2009, the market continues to be a neighborhood hub and destination for fresh food and cultural events.

Check out unique works of art crafted by some of DC's best local artists at Eastern Market!

Eastern Market
Inset: Southwest Waterfront
Detail: Arts and crafts, Eastern Market

Ornaments of nature occupy D.C.

EARLY ON, THE COUNTRY'S FOUNDERS recognized the importance of plants to the planet and its creatures. Not only are plants beautiful, they are also vital to our survival, providing food, oxygen, and medicines. The U.S. Botanic Garden and the National Arboretum are living educational and research museums that preserve and celebrate the wealth of plant species in our world.

Kenilworth Aquatic Gardens, on the banks of the Anacostia, have one of the world's largest displays of water lilies and aquatic plants.

Orchids, U.S. Botanic Garden
Inset: National Arboretum Children's Garden
Details: Water lilies, Kenilworth Aquatic Gardens

THE WHITE HOUSE HAS BEEN HOME to U.S. presidents and their families for over 200 years. George Washington was the only president who did not live there. Working from the Oval Office in the West Wing, the president is head of the government's executive branch. The White House bears the mark of many First Families who have expanded and improved it over time.

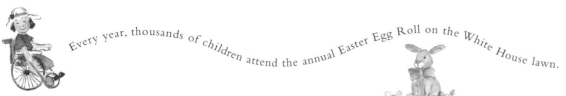

Every year, thousands of children attend the annual Easter Egg Roll on the White House lawn.

The White House
Inset: Oval Office, West Wing
Details: Easter Egg Roll, South Lawn

Quantities of coal moved more quickly by canal.

IN THE LATE 1790S AND EARLY 1800S, canals were built to speed the shipment of goods from eastern ports to the newly expanding West. Mules, sometimes guided by children, pulled boats through a series of locks that adjusted water levels. Canals were soon replaced by quick and more efficient railroads. The C&O (Chesapeake & Ohio) Canal, stretching 184.5 miles from Georgetown to Cumberland, Maryland, has been preserved as a national historic park.

C&O Canal, Georgetown
Inset: Lockkeeper's house, the Mall
Details: Boatman's instruments

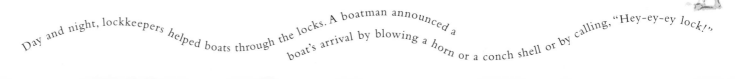
Day and night, lockkeepers helped boats through the locks. A boatman announced a boat's arrival by blowing a horn or a conch shell or by calling, "Hey-ey-ey lock!"

Rangers are resources for research and recreation.

 ESTABLISHED FOR THE ENJOYMENT AND BENEFIT of Americans in 1890, Rock Creek Park inspired the creation of future national parks. Stretching over 2,000 acres, the park is a natural oasis from city life, inviting visitors to explore its Nature Center and planetarium, ride horses, visit historic sites, and exercise. As in all the country's National Park Service areas, which today number more than 370, rangers lead educational tours, preserve natural and historic scenery, and protect wildlife for future generations.

Many animals make their home in Rock Creek Park.

Peirce Mill, Rock Creek Park
Inset: Rock Creek Park Horse Center
Details: Rock Creek Park inhabitants

Smithsonian scientists study and store specimens.

KENNETH E. BEHRING FAMILY ROTUNDA

Native Cultures of the Americas IMAX THEATER

↓ MUSEUM SHOPS CAFE

Pacific Cultures Asian Cultures African Cultures

THE SMITHSONIAN INSTITUTION, consisting of nineteen museums and the National Zoo, is the world's largest museum and research complex. Originally housed only in the "castle" on the National Mall, the Smithsonian was founded with a $500,000 bequest from Englishman James Smithson, who wanted to create "an establishment for the increase and diffusion of knowledge" in Washington, D.C. Often called the "nation's attic," the museum can show only about 2 percent of its holdings at one time.

Rotunda, National Museum of Natural History
Inset: Behind the scenes
Details: Smithsonian treasures

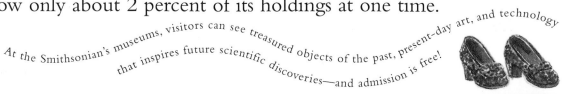

At the Smithsonian's museums, visitors can see treasured objects of the past, present-day art, and technology that inspires future scientific discoveries—and admission is free!

T rumpets play taps in tribute.

HERE RESTS IN
HONORED GLORY
AN AMERICAN
SOLDIER
KNOWN BUT TO GOD

FROM DECORATED GENERALS TO UNKNOWN SOLDIERS, the men and women buried at Arlington National Cemetery are honored for service to their country. On 624 acres surrounding Robert E. Lee's Arlington home lie the remains of veterans from every war the country has fought. Ceremonies here are traditional and formal: horses pull flag-draped coffins at solemn military funerals, and the guard changes in a precise ritual every half-hour or hour at the Tomb of the Unknowns.

Stones from his beloved Cape Cod surround the eternal flame at John F. Kennedy's grave.

Tomb of the Unknowns, Arlington National Cemetery
Inset: Horse stables, Fort Myers
Detail: Grave of John F. Kennedy

U Street's upbeat tempo unites the community.

DURING THE FIRST HALF OF THE 1900s, the U Street corridor was a bustling cultural and business neighborhood for Washington's African American population. Opened in 1921, the Lincoln Theater became a community centerpiece, attracting big-name jazz singers like Duke Ellington, Billie Holiday, and Ella Fitzgerald. The area fell into decline after the 1960s, but it has been revitalized since the 1994 reopening and loving restoration of the Lincoln Theater.

Ben's Chili Bowl, U Street
Inset: Duke Ellington, U Street
Details: Howard University

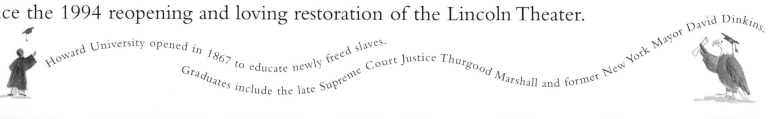

Howard University opened in 1867 to educate newly freed slaves. Graduates include the late Supreme Court Justice Thurgood Marshall and former New York Mayor David Dinkins.

Veterans' memorials reflect valor.

THE VIETNAM VETERANS MEMORIAL, designed by Maya Ying Lin, is inscribed with the names of more than 58,000 people who died in the Vietnam War. "Freedom Is Not Free" are the words on the wall of the Korean War Veterans Memorial. Both memorials have helped the process of national healing by honoring the great courage and sacrifice of the men and women who have fought to preserve democracy in recent history.

Veterans Day services, parades, and wreath-laying ceremonies commemorate U.S. military personnel who have lost their lives at war.

Vietnam Veterans Memorial
Inset: Korean War Veterans Memorial
Detail: Memorial wreath

World War II awakened the world.

NEVER FORGET

REMEMBER

HOLOCAUST

CHARTREUSE

I'm TURQUOISE

THAT'S GREAT

We Remember

HOPE

What's so Funny 'Bout

PEACE LOVE UNDERSTANDING

PEACE JOY

JOIN HANDS

ALL PEOPLE ARE CREATED EQUAL

NEVER AGAIN

In a time of terror, Love will keep us together.

FRIENDSHIP

PACIFIC   PACIFIC

OPENED IN 1993, the U.S. Holocaust Memorial Museum tells the stories of millions of Jews and "undesirables" killed by the Nazis between 1933 and 1945. When Japan bombed Pearl Harbor in December 1941, the United States entered World War II, fighting against Imperial Japan and Nazi Germany. The new National World War II Memorial honors all those who served during the war, and acknowledges the nation's commitment to protect worldwide peace and freedom.

WWII Memorial
Inset: The Wall of Remembrance, Holocaust Memorial Museum
Detail: Iwo Jima Statue, Arlington, Virginia

The Iwo Jima Memorial recreates Joe Rosenthal's Pulitzer Prize–winning photo of the U.S. flag being raised on a battle site in Asia where over 5,000 marines died.

eXhibits help prevent eXtinction.

THE SMITHSONIAN HOUSED ITS FIRST LIVE ANIMALS on the Mall. Congress established the National Zoo in 1889 after space became crowded. Committed to the study, celebration, and protection of animals and their natural habitats, it has become one of the world's leading research zoos. The popular pandas Mei Xiang and Tian Tian help raise awareness of all endangered species.

The National Zoo's newly opened "Elephant Trails" offers Asian elephants and their offspring even more room to roam!

Pandas, National Zoo
Inset: Bald Eagle Refuge, National Zoo
Detail: Elephant Trails, National Zoo

Youngsters explore days of yore.

Great Falls Park
Maryland
Turkey Run Farm
Clara Barton National Historic Site
Glen Echo Park
Claude Moore Farm
Washington D.C.
Fort Marcy
Theodore Roosevelt Island
U.S. Marine Corps War Memorial
Lady Bird Johnson Park
LBJ Memorial
Arlington House
Navy & Marine Memorial
Arlington National Cemetery
Virginia
Roaches Run
Gravelly Point
Dangerfield Island
Alexandria
Jones Point Lighthouse
Belle Haven Park
Dyke Marsh Wildlife Preserve
Collingwood Picnic Area
Fort Hunt Park
Riverside Park
Mount Vernon

HISTORY IS BROUGHT TO LIFE at many sites in and around Washington, D.C. George Washington's estate, Mount Vernon, offers a peek into the operations of a colonial farm. From the estate, families can visit historic sites along the George Washington Memorial Parkway. On tours at the Daughters of the American Revolution Museum, in downtown Washington, children wear old-fashioned clothes and play with colonial toys.

Mount Vernon, Fairfax County, Virginia
Inset: George Washington Memorial Parkway
Details: "Sunday toys," DAR Museum

Noah's arks and fancy china dolls were "Sunday toys" in colonial times. Children could play with them quietly only on this one day of the week.

Zip codes zoom mail to distant zones.

BENJAMIN FRANKLIN

THROUGHOUT HISTORY, the U.S. Postal Service has been one of the strongest ties binding the nation. The need to deliver news quickly has continually challenged the postal service to push the frontiers of transportation technology from post riders to overnight air delivery. Benjamin Franklin, joint postmaster general for the American colonies, brought order to the mails in 1753. His statue greets visitors to the National Postal Museum.

In 1916, letter carriers who hand-delivered mail complained that people took too long to answer their doors. Now every house must have either a mailbox or a letter slot.

Wells Fargo Stagecoach, National Postal Museum
Inset: Ben Franklin statue, National Postal Museum
Detail: "To Mom, with Love"

Keep your eye on the grand old flag!

Dinosaur

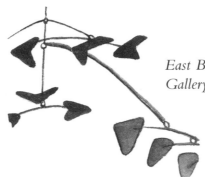

East Building, National
Gallery of Art

Frederick Douglass
House

Inaugural Gown

First Woman US Supreme Court Justice

"Necessary,"
Mount Vernon

Owney,
Postal Service
Mascot

Pentagon

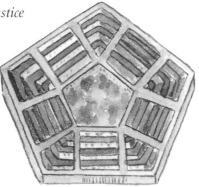

Senate Soup

Teddy Bear

Xmas Time

Yummy!

Zschock

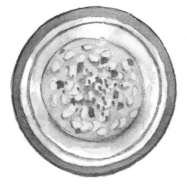

American Beauty

Bird

*Carousel,
Glen Echo Park*

*Giant,
Haines Point*

Hopscotch

Kite Festival

*Lichtenstein,
Sculpture Garden*

Mary McLeod Bethune

Quill Pen

Row House

Uncle Sam

Vendor

*West Building,
National Gallery
of Art*